The Smarter Home Office:

8 simple steps to increase your income, inspiration and comfort

Linda Varone

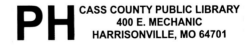
5/11

the smarter home office:

8 simple steps to increase your income, inspiration and comfort

Linda Varone, MA

Great Meadows Publishing

the smarter home office:
8 simple steps to increase your income, inspiration and comfort
Linda Varone

Published by
Great Meadows Publishing
10 Old Colony Lane
Arlington, Ma 02476

Library of Congress Control Number: 2010904220

ISBN: 978-0-9844045-06

Special thanks to Ann Cantalupa, Marilee Driscoll, Dennis Mahoney, Michele Meagher, Lillian Rehder, Margy Rydzynski, Judy Osborne, Elise Pepe, Becky Sarah and Rae Simpson.
Without you this book would not exist.

For Mom
Alice Jensen Varone
1912-2004
Who taught me the joy in simple things.

Do you have a love/hate relationship with your home office?

Do you feel:

- Cramped?
- Disorganized?
- Invaded?
- Isolated?
- Bored?
- Distracted?
- Tired?

The Smarter Home Office : 8 simple steps to increase your income, inspiration and comfort solves these problems and helps you improve your workflow, organization and comfort. This book will show you the surprisingly simple steps to set-up or rearrange your home office for increased efficiency, comfort and personal inspiration

Contents

Introduction:
If Your Home is Your Castle.
Why Does Your Office Feel Like a Dungeon?

"It's not inviting."

"I don't make time to go in there. It feels like a death sentence."

Create a dream home office of your own.

Imagine yourself entering your office. Sunlight falls on your desktop. You ease into a comfortable chair at your desk. Your computer is humming and your keyboard is positioned so your wrists, arms and shoulders are relaxed. You reach for your phone and headset. You glance out the window to your side and glimpse trees and sky. You touch the leaf of a lush green plant on your desk. You look beyond your computer screen at a picture of your favorite place in the world and smile. You swivel your chair and open a drawer to select the paperwork you are currently focused on. After working for a while and in need of a break from your desk, you pick up your paperwork and move to a comfortable upholstered chair in a corner by the window, maintaining the flow of your work while getting away from the desk. You place your coffee mug on a table next to your reading chair and reach up to turn on a nearby lamp. You look up and see a picture of the inspiration for your hard work: your dream home, your dream vacation, your children.

1

The Home Office Dungeon

Many home offices mimic the layout and impersonality of the typical cubicle: a desk pushed against a blank wall with a computer, printer, phone, chair and file cabinet, all illuminated with a 60-watt bulb in a ceiling fixture. This is bare, and barely functional. And, to add insult to injury, this bland room is adorned with piles of papers. The worst of both worlds.

In this office everything ends up on the floor because there is inadequate storage and work surfaces.

Another type of dysfunctional home office has no "home" of its own. The laptop and cell phone migrate from place-to-place and papers are scattered around several rooms. Working at a dining or coffee table is never comfortable and valuable time is wasted searching from room to room for a particular file. And, when it's dinner time or guests appear, you have to pack up and remove your work – more inconvenience, more disruption.

Your office needs to fit you and your work style. The problems you have experienced in working at home may have less to do with will power than with the set-up of your work space. The best technology in the world will help, but not guarantee, your success. A beautiful antique desk may delight your aesthetic sense, but

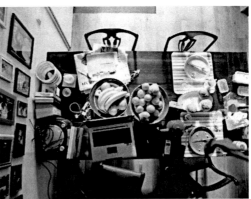

A laptop amid the crumbs is a make-do office.

ignores the fact you work with a computer, not a quill pen. Technology and aesthetics by themselves overlook the human factor in designing a successful office.

The Smarter Home Office: 8 Simple Steps to Increase Your Income, Inspiration and Comfort will show you, step-by-step, how to make your home office generate more income by increasing your comfort (no distracting headaches), efficiency (what you need is a chair swivel away), and inspiration (an office that is personal and welcoming).

> The problems you experience working at home may have less to do with will power than with the set-up of your work space.

Whether you are self-employed, a telecommuter, a work-at-home-mom, or are writing your dissertation or a novel, your office is a reflection of your professional image and aspirations. Even if you are the only one who sees it, it speaks volumes to your subconscious. If your office is messy and thrown together your space drags you down, if it is merely functional you avoid it altogether. If your office is neat, efficient, and comfortable (yes, comfortable), it supports you as a professional who is focused, smart and productive. Add personalization and inspiration to keep your goals and dreams in mind. Making these improvements does not take a lot of money. It *does* take innovative thinking, something you use all the time.

> Even if you are the only one who sees it, your office speaks volumes to your subconscious.

The Smarter Home Office: 8 Simple Steps to Increase Your Income, Inspiration and Comfort focuses on the human factor, *you*. This book guides you, to set up a room that makes your work easier by rethinking how your desk and

3

work storage are laid out, adding appropriate lighting, and placing artwork and plants to create *your* dream corner office.

Having helped clients arrange their homes and offices since 1991, I have witnessed the love/hate relationship people have with their home office, People like you have shared their strong feelings: love the commute, but hate the clutter; love the personal space, but hate the isolation. At the same time, you have limited space, time and money for making improvements. Recognizing these challenges *The Smarter Home Office* gives you real-life solutions that are surprisingly simple.

While most of *The Smarter Home Office* is focused on the home office, many of the solutions here can be used to improve corporate offices.

This book is based on my experience working with a wide variety of clients, my background in both architectural psychology (the overlooked human factor in design), interior design, and the results of an anonymous (and very candid) survey with over 250 respondents (some of whose comments are at the beginning of each chapter). **My goal is to help you create a home office that supports your work style and your goals, while respecting the realities of your time, space and budget.**

"Order, comfort and connection"
– survey respondent's goals for her home office.

The eight steps described here are surprisingly simple, practical, and low-cost.
- Arrange furniture to support your personal work flow.

- Adjust your furniture for ergonomic ease.
- Add lighting to comfortably illuminate your desk
- Tap into the calming and energizing power of nature.
- Set the mood with color for focus or activity.
- Discover room for a home office in underused or overlooked spaces.
- Maximize storage.
- Inspire and motivate yourself with personal mementos.

This book offers you ideas to use and play with to create a home office that works for you. As with the best jazz or cooking, improvisation is strongly encouraged.

Step #1
Furniture Arrangement:
The Antidote to Cubicle Think
and Grad Student Sprawl

"The printer takes up too much room on my desk"

"I would love a large work table to spread out on."

"I'm using cast-off furniture that doesn't work with the space."

Arrange your office to support your work flow and work style.

One of my clients has a large sunny home office, but his desk was squeezed into a dark back corner. He had unconsciously created a "home office cubicle." We turned it around and moved it next to the window. Now natural light illuminates his desk, his files are easier to access and he can look out the window and see his children playing.

Desk Set-Ups to Improve Your Work Flow

Your desk is the single most important piece of furniture in your office, but many people have desks that are too small for their work. This is supported by the responses to my survey: people either loved or despaired about their desks. In that light, consider this factoid: The information crossing your desk has increased by 600%, while the size of your desktop is 37% smaller. Your desktop needs to be large enough to support your work style with room for your computer, phone, printer *and* your paperwork. The size of the standard office (not cubicle) desk is 60 to 72 inches wide and 30 to 36 inches

7

deep. What I often see in clients' home offices and furniture catalogues are desks from 31 - 47 inches wide and 20 - 25 inches deep.

Computer desks, "student" desks and decorator desks have just enough room for your computer monitor or laptop, while ignoring your real world need for a phone, printer and papers, let alone your feet and legs. This leads to "make-do" arrangements – such as printers precariously balanced on TV tray tables. A too-small desk leads to the stacking and scattering of necessary papers, making work more inefficient and stressful. And many "computer desks" lack room for the wrist support essential to good ergonomics (more on this in Step #2.)

A computer desk is a storage unit by another name.

A heavily promoted space waster is the storage "hutch" often seen on desks, those 2-foot tall, 8-inch deep arrangements of cubbies and drawers. They are great in theory, but are too shallow for real storage and take up valuable desktop real estate.

The desk hutch wastes valuable desktop real estate.

Your desk is the hub of your office. You want everything arranged around you and easy to reach, with the most frequently used items just an arm's reach or chair swivel away. The solution is either a larger desk, an "L" shaped desk, or creating a "working L": two desks or a desk and a table at right angles to each other to support improved work flow. This reference desk or "L" can be as shallow as 15 inches deep. To accommodate this side table you will need to have your main desk away from the wall to allow you to open the desk

The "L" desk supports work flow.

drawers. Place your computer monitor or laptop on one desk or table and your papers, reference and writing materials on the other. If you work at your side table or desk, make sure there is room for your feet and legs.

Create a "working L" of your own with a desk and side table or credenza.

The "working galley" has work surfaces in front and back.

An alternative arrangement is to have a lateral file credenza or bookcase behind you, either in addition to the "L" desk arrangement or creating a "working galley".

Desk Location

The ideal position for your desk is perpendicular to a window

When arranging furniture in your office start with your desk, the largest piece of furniture and the place where you will be spending most of your time. Many people reflexively position their desk up against a wall or install a built-in desk

9

along a wall. Don't recreate the boxed-in feeling of a cubicle in you home office.

The ideal position for your desk is near a window – perpendicular to the window works best – to take advantage of natural light, to minimize glare on or around your computer screen and to avoid being distracted by the outside view.

Position your desk facing the door to greet clients.

Many of us are inspired by the rooms we see on television or in the movies. Sometimes a desk will be positioned so the actor looks directly out a window. It looks professional…and romantic. But in reality, the desk was positioned to facilitate camera angles, not the character's writing.

If clients come to your office, place your desk so you can see the door when they enter. This allows you to welcome them and set the tone of your interaction. If your home office is for you only, then arrange your desk to take advantage of natural light. If you feel more comfortable facing the door, then place your desk accordingly. If you must place your desk and/or computer with your back to a door, then consider mounting a small mirror on your monitor to act as a rear view mirror. This addresses the hard-wired human response of becoming tense or vigilant when your back is exposed. Do what feels right for you.

A computer monitor mirror helps you relax and focus if your back is to the door.

There is no need for you and your desk to be tethered to an inferior location by cable, phone or electrical outlets – that is what extension cords are for.

10

Your Desk Chair

The second most important piece of furniture in your office is your desk chair. We will discuss this in detail in Step 2, the ergonomics chapter.

The Best Home Office Perk: The Reading Chair

Sitting at a desk for hours on end can be very tiring. Fatigue impairs your productivity and concentration. You need a change, while maintaining your work momentum.

One of the great perks of working at home is the comfortable upholstered reading chair. Place it near a window with a lamp close by for easy reading and a small table for your coffee cup or tea mug and

Take a break from your desk and keep working in your office reading chair.

papers. Having a reading chair in your office allows you to give your back a rest and literally get a new perspective on what you are doing. If the chair is near a window, connect with nature for a while. The reading chair is not limited to the home office. If you have space in your corporate office, add a comfortable chair with the accoutrements of work nearby.

An alternative to the reading chair is the reading sofa. This is perfect if you like to stretch out when reading. A sofa bed in a home office/guest room serves two functions. Make sure there is good lighting nearby. More about lighting in Step #3.

Take a look at what furniture you are currently working with. Are you making do with deflated chair cushions, file drawers that do not fully open and an old desk lamp from your college days? If so, it is time to update your office furniture and accessories. You need furniture that functions effortlessly, while supporting your body and your work. If your file cabinet does not open smoothly, then you are less likely to file your papers, and they end up all over the place. A desk chair with tired cushions or broken adjustment levers can cause pain and fatigue. An old lamp may no longer give you the efficient light you need. A budget-appropriate investment in office furniture that supports your work is money well spent.

With office furniture (as with anything) expensive is easy, cheap and shoddy is easy, but reasonably priced and good quality is hard to find. While there is no direct correlation between price and quality, cheap office furniture can mean cutting corners with poor materials or construction that will not last. Let comfort and function guide your choices. Take the time to get the best furniture for your money.

Highlights
- Use a desk large enough for your needs and your electronics.
- Position your desk near a window.
- Align your desk perpendicular to the window.
- Use an L-shaped desk or create a "working L."
- Place your desk to see the door, or use a computer monitor mirror.
- If you have the space, set up a comfortable reading chair.

On the left is a corporate office cubicle and on the right is a home office cubicle. Not much difference. Don't reflexively push your desk against the wall. In your own office take advantage of your space and freedom

"We moved our desk by the window. I can't believe how different it feels in there now."
- client

Step #2
Ergonomics Made Easy:
The Secret Factor in Productivity

"My cheap chairs don't really work for me."

"My chair looks good but is not comfortable."

"I am thinking of a standing desk."

Ergonomics prevents your work becoming a "pain in the neck."

Wayne, a tall, lean athlete-entrepreneur, had a home office with all the latest technical gadgets, but he usually worked on his laptop at the kitchen counter. A little detective work revealed that his desk chair, which he had owned "forever," had slowly, imperceptibly died: the height adjustment no longer worked. His chair now fit his young daughter. No wonder he worked in the kitchen! We found an adjustable chair scaled for taller people and now he works comfortably and effectively in his home office.

Comfort = Productivity
Many people think office ergonomics is too complicated and too expensive to tackle. Executed in a rigid way it can be, but if you approach it with a bit of common sense it is easy to do. Most office ergonomics simply involve adjusting your chair, your keyboard and/or your monitor. A few minutes of fine-tuning your set-up will pay benefits in reduced neck, shoulder, back and wrist strain.

15

The Ergonomic Equation (with apologies to Albert Einstein)

Sitting at a desk or computer for long hours can be very fatiguing. If your body is not in natural, supported alignment you can experience back pain, sore muscles, headache and eye strain.

A simple way to remember ergonomics is:
E^2 = MCK
Ergonomics made Easy = Monitor (or laptop screen) + Chair + Keyboard.

Monitor height

Keyboard height

Chair height

Feet supported on floor or footrest

Adjust your monitor, keyboard and chair height for comfort and support.

Starting from the ground up:
    1. Chair
A chair by itself is not the solution to back problems, regardless of its price. To prevent leg cramps and back pain your desk chair must:
- Allow your feet to rest flat on the floor, and
- Adjust so your ankles, knees and hips are at approximately 90° or right angles.

Your chair is part of the ergonomic equation.

Avoid laptop hunch.

Adjust your keyboard tray to a level that allows your shoulders to relax.

2. Keyboard

Hunched shoulders are a major source of muscle tension. Extended use of a laptop on a table or standard height desk can result in the forward rounding of shoulders and upper back pain. What can you do to avoid this?

- Use a standard keyboard and mouse connected to your laptop, placed on a keyboard tray or adjustable stand.
- Adjust the height of your keyboard so it allows your shoulders to relax, your elbows at a 90° angle and your forearms parallel to the floor.
- The keyboard tray or drawer should be wide enough to hold your computer mouse as well. This allows you to easily move your hand and forearm back and forth between keyboard and mouse.
- Center the QWERTY section of your keyboard with your monitor screen, not the entire keyboard, This prevents a subtle but fatiguing twisting of your shoulders.
- Crucial: Place a wrist support cushion below your keyboard AND mouse.
- Newer desks designed for home offices have a keyboard drawer at a comfortable and ergonomic height. See if this works for you. If not, you may need an articulating keyboard tray or adjustable keyboard stand.

3. Monitor or Laptop Screen

To avoid neck pain and headaches have your computer screen adjusted so your head is balanced without being thrust forward or tilted back.

17

- Twisting to see your monitor is a set-up for back problems. Have your computer screen and keyboard aligned right in front of you.
- Ergonomic engineers recommend adjusting your computer monitor so the top of the computer screen is level with your eyes. This allows for a

Bi-focal head-tilt results in a stiff neck. A slanted or off-center monitor screen results in back pain.

slightly downward gaze that is less fatiguing for your eyes and can minimize dry eyes (because your eyes are not wide open.)
- You may need an adjustable monitor or laptop stand or simply a box, phone book or ream of paper to elevate your computer screen.
- If you are short when seated or wear bi-focals, you may need to lower your computer screen, so you do not have to tilt your head back to read the text on the screen.
- The screen itself should be about an arm's length from where you are sitting.
- If you find yourself squinting or leaning forward or back to see better, you might want to use the often overlooked "zoom" function on your computer's tool bar or hit <Ctrl> and move your mouse roller ball to make the screen easier to read. Or the solution can be as simple as moving the monitor or laptop screen a few inches closer to you.

Use variations on these recommendations to make your workspace supportive and comfortable for you.
- If you are short you may need an angled foot rest to provide a solid surface for your feet while your chair is raised to align comfortably with your keyboard tray.
- If you are short you may not need to elevate your computer screen.

- If you are tall you may need a custom desk or one with adjustable legs to provide more knee room.
- If you are very tall you may need to use either a standing desk or a drafting table as your desk with a drafting stool or chair (without its foot rest) to comfortably accommodate your longer legs and torso.

In your home office *you* decide how to make your desk, chair and monitor *fit you*.

The Standing Desk: Take a Break from Back Pain

For some people with chronic low back pain a standing desk can be very helpful, either as your main desk or a "break" desk. A standing desk was famously used by Ernest Hemingway because of an old back injury. There are no hard and fast rules for measurements for standing desks. Simply follow the recommendations above for support of your wrists and keeping your shoulders relaxed while your forearms are parallel to the floor and your elbows at right angles. If you use an adjustable desk that converts to a standing desk, simply play around with the height adjustments. If you decide on a custom standing desk, set up some boxes with your keyboard and monitor on them until you have a comfortable arrangement and then take measurements. Place a gel or air-cushioned floor mat, or a thick rug where you stand at your desk. Your feet will thank you.

The standing desk - an old idea meets modern needs.

What to Look For in a New Desk Chair

You can cut corners elsewhere, but make sure that your desk chair is adjustable, supportive and fits *you*.

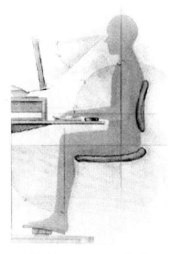

- The chair seat should be shallow enough for your feet to be flat on the floor while your back is supported.
- The chair seat should be deep enough to support the length of your thighs without the front edge of the seat pressing into the back of your knees.
- For safety, your rolling desk chair should have a five-point base.
- Make sure there is lumbar support in the chair back and that it aligns with your own lumbar area.

Make sure your chair provides lumbar support and the seat edge does not cut into the back of your knees.

Tip: Always do a "sit test" on any chair you are thinking of buying. After you have adjusted all the levers and knobs on the chair, just sit in it for several minutes to focus in on how you feel. Take your time; you will spend a lot of time in this chair if you buy it.

Pretend you are sitting at your desk and hold your arms and hands in a realistic keyboard position. From the top down, are your shoulders, elbows, wrists and hands, hips, knees and feet in proper ergonomic alignment? If yes and you feel supported and comfortable you have found your chair. Save the really cushy chairs for your home office reading chair.

Please don't do this to your back.

Telephone Headset

Telephone headsets prevent neck and shoulder strain.

If you do a lot of telephoning or do extended telephone interviews, you may want to consider a telephone headset that can be connected to your desktop or cellular phones. Headsets are relatively inexpensive and save you the cost of visits to your chiropractor. One client told me, with a smile, that she uses a two ear-piece headphone to screen out the distracting noise of her kids.

Highlights
- Comfort = Productivity.
- Adjust your computer screen, keyboard and chair so your shoulders are relaxed and your elbows, hips and knees are at approximately 90° angles.
- Wrist support is crucial.
- Consider a standing desk if you need a break from sitting.
- If you are buying a new chair get one that fits you - seat depth, lumbar support and feet flat on the floor.
- If you are on the phone much of the time, consider a telephone headset..

Step #3
Lighting:
Illuminate Your World

"My office is dark and messy"

"I need more natural light."

"How can I find a better desk lamp?"

Fluorescent lighting can look institutional and cause eye strain.

A client was troubled by severe migraines triggered by fluorescent lighting. We turned off the overhead fluorescent panels and placed a table lamp with an incandescent (Edison) bulb on her desk and another on the file credenza behind her. "My migraines disappeared!" she excitedly told me.

Many clients overlook the importance of good lighting to establish a comfortable and efficient office. They use inadequate or inappropriate artificial lighting, ignore the natural light available to them, and then wonder why their home office is dark and uninviting. Human beings are instinctively drawn to light. Use this instinctive response to light to make your office more welcoming for you and your clients.

How to Access Natural Light

Natural light is the best light. You can access natural light with a window, a skylight or a solar tube.

Position your desk near a window to get the most sunlight.

If possible, position your desk near a window. This will give you natural light for at least part of the day. Then position your desk *perpendicular* to the window. This allows natural light to illuminate your work surface and avoids extreme light contrasts and looking into sun glare.

If sunlight fills your office, you are all set. If you have sun for only part of the day, need to close your window shades against too-bright sunlight, have dreary overcast days, or work before sunrise or after sunset, you need supplemental artificial light.

The Smart Use of Artificial Light

A simple change in lighting can be one of the most powerful yet cost-effective changes you make in your home office.

Assess the artificial light in your home office. Do you have a lamp on your desk, near your reading chair, or behind you? Often I see home offices with only a ceiling fixture. Ceiling mounted light – whether it is recessed, track lighting, or a single fixture – is not adequate for illuminating your home office. Light coming from your ceiling will run out of illuminating energy (called *foot candles*) by the time it reaches your desk or chair. You need lighting near you, like a table or floor lamp that casts its light on your paperwork.

Desk lamps with opaque shades create extremes of brightness and darkness.

Most people think of a desk lamp as the perfect lighting for an office. But desk lamps, by design, create a circle of very bright light with darkness

24

beyond that. This contrast between extreme light and dark causes eye strain. When your eyes get tired, you become tired. Desk lamps were designed for architects when they worked with pencil and paper to a scale
of ¼ inch or less. Save your desk lamp for detailed work.

I recommend you borrow a lighting idea from the executive suite. Use table lamps on your desk. A table lamp, with a white or off-white

A table lamp gives you the best light for working by your reading chair or at your desk.

translucent shade, softly diffuses the light and prevents the sharp, fatiguing demarcation between light and dark on your desk top. Plus, it looks professional. A good rule of thumb is to have the bottom of the lamp shade a bit taller than the top of your monitor or computer screen. The taller the lamp, the larger the circle of light on your work surface. Translucent lamp shades, in white or off-white, allow the most light to spread in a larger circle while softly diffusing the light. Diffused light is easier on the eyes and makes
the room – and you – more attractive.

Most people work best if there are two sources of light in a home office: two lamps, a lamp and natural light, or overhead light and a table lamp.

Incandescent vs. Fluorescent Lighting: The Flicker Factor, or Why Fluorescent Light Can Cause Headaches and Eye Fatigue

I generally recommend incandescent (Edison-type) light bulbs over fluorescent lighting, whether tube or compact fluorescent. Incandescent light works by electricity flowing into a filament inside the light bulb. This flow of electricity makes the filament white hot, creating heat and unvarying light. Fluorescent lighting, including compact fluorescents, operates by electrically exciting a gas that is sealed inside the tube or bulb. This in turn makes the phosphor coating on the inside of the glass tube glow. The mixture of phosphors coating the glass determines the warmth or coolness of the light. The electricity that activates the fluorescent light pulses on and off 50-60 times a second. This is too fast for us to see, consciously. Research in the last few decades has discovered the eye-brain connection allows people to subconsciously see and remember things viewed in only a milli-second; which is much faster than 60 times a second. Therefore, we subconsciously see fluorescent light flicker on and off, but are not aware of it. This could contribute to the eye fatigue and headaches so many people suffer after a work day under acres of fluorescent panels. Incandescent light bulbs do not have this flicker factor. A lamp with an incandescent bulb or consistent sunlight can off-set the effect of fluorescent lighting.

The right compact fluorescent bulb makes your office more welcoming.

Not All Compact Fluorescents are Created Equal

Fluorescents are a fact of life. But you may dis-like the light quality of compact fluorescent lights (CFLs), feeling it is harsh or cold, giving your office an institutional look. Compact fluorescents are not any brighter than compar-able incandescent bulbs, but the color of the light is different: cooler and whiter. Incandes-cent (Edison) light bulbs create light that is warmer and perceived by many people as more welcoming. In the last few years manufacturers have made available CFLs that have a warmer, more incandescent quality to them. Look for la-bels that say "warm white" or "soft white." Avoid CFLs that are labeled "cool white" or "bright white."

Tip: Full Spectrum light is a cooler, bluer form of light.

It approximates the light of a blue sky. Full Spectrum light is not a cure-all lighting solution. It is best used as focused task lighting for extended reading or fine craft work.

Computer Screen Glare Solutions

If you experience light glare on your computer screen, adjust the tilt of the screen and turn off any lights that shine down on your screen. Or use one of the polarized anti-glare or anti-reflective screens or optical coatings.

Highlights

More does not mean better. The *right* lighting makes your home office welcoming and

- Position your work surface near a window to make the most of sunlight.
- Use a table lamp on your desk with a white translucent shade.
- Have a second source of light in your office.
- If you work under fluorescent lighting only, consider using a lamp with an incandescent bulb to avoid "flicker factor."
- If you use fluorescent light, use "warm white" or "soft white" light bulbs.
- Full spectrum light is best used for extended reading or fine craft work.

Step #4
The Power of Nature:
De-stress and Energize Yourself

A client complained about his lifeless home office. I suggested he move a few plants into the room. "I love my plants. I just never thought of bringing them into my office. They make the room come alive."

"I have no windows in my home office."

"My plants add so much to my office."

"I love the view of city roof tops from my window."

If you worked in a cubicle farm or crowded office, you probably had little or no access to nature. But in your home office you can change that. Why is contact with nature so important? A growing number of studies are documenting the fact that contact with nature decreases both acute and chronic stress and decreases the incidence of illness.

Nature and elegance.

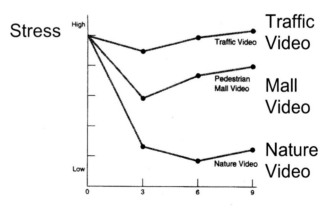

The most dramatic, sustained decrease in blood pressure occurred when test subjects viewed a nature video.

A window is your direct connection with nature.

The most direct way to connect with nature in your home office is to place your desk or reading chair near a window to enjoy sunlight and views. If you live in a city, then you can glimpse the amazing variety of street life in your neighborhood. If your view is limited then enjoy the change of light as the sun and clouds move across the sky. Looking out your window for a minute or two will rest your eyes and your mind.

Curtains, Shades, Blinds or Nothing: How and When to Frame Your View.

Windows are your main access to nature when indoors. Sometimes that connect-
ion is unintentionally limited by curtains or other window treatments. There are only four reasons for window treatments:

1. Protection from sun glare and heat.
2. Protection from cold.
3. Protection from an unattractive view.
4. Protection from nosey neighbors.

If none of these situations apply to you, consider a curtain-free or minimally "dressed" window.

Bottom-up shades give you privacy with views of the sky.

Hint: Bottom-up shades can give you privacy with views of sun, sky, and tree tops.

How to Frame Your View with Curtains

If a room looks unfinished to you without curtains, here are some tips.
• Just as you frame a picture, window treatments should frame rather than upstage your view.

- Use curtain rods at least 12 inches wider than the window frame, 6 inches or more beyond each frame edge. Then when you pull back the curtains they will frame your view, not block a third of it.
- Hang your curtain rod close to the ceiling; this will make the window appear taller and bigger.
- Simple is best.

Open a window for a cooling breeze or to draw in some energizing fresh air. As a bonus you may hear birdsong or rustling leaves.

Reminder: Dirty windows can sneak up on you. Keep your windows clean to make the most of your light and view.

Bring Elements of Nature Indoors

Bring nature indoors to brighten your home office. I encourage you to have a live plant on your desk, if you have the room and the right light. Something simple is fine. Fresh cut flowers are a special delight. If you feel helpless in the presence of a live plant; then *good quality* silk flowers or plants are the next best thing. An aquarium can be fun. If you have a pet who quietly keeps you company while you work, you are truly blessed. At the very least, hang a picture of your favorite outdoor place where you can easily see it.

Bring living things into your work space.

Highlights
- Contact with nature decreases stress.
- Windows are your main access to nature when indoors.
- How you frame your windows can make or break your view.
- Bring elements of nature indoors.

Step #5
Color Confidence:
How to Choose the Best Color
for Your Work Style

"I can't find a wall color I like."

"I want a new color."

"My walls are still white."

Several years ago, I was helping a client set up a home office for her extensive volunteer work. She wanted something other than boring beige on the walls, but was unsure what color was "right." When she looked at an array of paint chips I had laid out for her, she lunged for two shades of green. Her face was shining as she held the paint chips for me to see. In that moment my client learned a new respect for her own intuition and inner wisdom. A few weeks later she called me: "I am sitting here in my new green room and I just love how it makes me feel."

Color has a powerful effect on how you feel and function in a space.

Factoid: Today there are over 16,000 paint colors to choose from, up from 400-600 in the 1990's. No wonder you are overwhelmed choosing colors for your office!

Color for Drama vs. Color for Living

Rooms on television or in print are decorated so they will have visual drama, but these same

Color choices are limitless. This can be good or overwhelming.

colors can be too strong to live with. Let your own response to a color guide you, rather than unquestioningly copying a color from a magazine or book. Save that dramatic color for an accent piece, a foyer, or a hallway that you move through but don't spend time in.

I recommend that you use wall colors that look like they come from nature. Some paint colors look "synthetic": too bright, too pale or too grayed down. Wall colors work best if they form a background for you and your personal decorations and activities, rather than colors and faux finishes that dominate a room.

Wall colors are best when they create a background for *you*.

How to Create a Color Environment: Match Your Wall Colors to Your Work Style

Match the energy of your home office colors with the energy you need for your work. There is no one "best" office color. Color is an important element in the visual stimulation of a room. You want to coordinate color response with the kind of work you do.

Colors for Activity

Bright warm colors such as yellow, orange and red stimulate activity. In a brightly illuminated room, yellow can stimulate creativity, conversation and movement. Rather than primary colors, use toned down versions of bright colors on your walls. That is, use either colors that are slightly paler than the boldest color on the paint fan leaf, or a more subdued version. This is great for brainstorming, rote tasks, and repetitive artisan work. If you work

Choose colors from nature, rather than ones that look unreal or

in sales, you may want bright colors on your walls to pump you up for cold calls.

Colors for Concentration

Medium to deep colors, such as some shades of blue or green, in a room with medium light levels stimulate inward focus and concentration. If your work is more analytical or reflective, then deeper colors may work better for you. To avoid a cave-like atmosphere with dark colors, you need more lighting, a white ceiling, and light neutral flooring and woodwork to balance the darker tones of the walls. Or you can choose a combination of deep or neutral colors on the wall with bright points of color in your artwork and accessories.

Whatever color you choose, make sure it is a color you love and then tweak the tone or intensity of the color to support your work style. Color is personal; try different combinations. What is right for *you* is the important thing.

Color + Light = Metamerism: The Key to Finding the Right Color

Color and light are inseparable. Different kinds of light can make the same paint chip look very different. This is called "metamerism" (me-**tam**-mer-ism). Fluorescent lighting in a paint store will make colors look paler and cooler than they really are. When that color goes on the wall it will look brighter and stronger than you intended. This may explain why your neighbor has a neon yellow house.

Color and light are inseparable. Different kinds of light can make the same paint chip look very different. This is called "metamerism."

35

The northern part of the U.S. tends to have "cool" sunlight. I recommend colors with a warm undertone to correct for this. Colors with a warm undertone appear to have a touch of brown or beige added, while colors with a cool undertone look like they have had some gray or pure white added. If you want to work with a blue, choose a blue with a warm quality such as periwinkle. If yellow is the color you love, find a yellow with a golden undertone. The American South and Southwest have a very warm intense sunlight. Bright colors can stand up to this light while paler colors can look washed out. Different parts of the country (and the world) have different kinds of sun light, so colors need to be selected where they will be used.

When selecting a color, take advantage of the sample pots of paint that are now available. Paint a patch on the wall or on an 18-inch by 18-inch poster board to really see the color; paint to the edges so the white board does not distort your color perception. Do this with several tones of a color to help you make a choice you will love. Always make your final color choice in the room you are going to paint.

Have fun and use colors you love.

Choosing the Right Paint

For paint finishes I recommend
- Eggshell finish on the walls for its low sheen and easy washability;
- Semi-Gloss for your woodwork for better washability; and
- White ceilings for simplicity and to reflect the light from your lamps.

You may not want or need the most expensive paint available, but the cheapest paints will cost you in time and energy – more paint and more coats for better coverage and depth of color. Aim for the best quality paint your time and money budget will allow.

Have fun and use colors you love.

Highlights

Always make your final color choice in the room you are going to paint.

- Wall colors are best when they create a background for you and your activities.
- Choose wall colors that support your work style.
- Understanding metamerism is the key to finding the right color.
- Always make your final color choice in the room you are painting.
- Select the best quality paint for your time and money budget.

Step #6
Dinosaur Space:
Break Loose from Room Labels

"It's dark, damp and lonely in the basement."

"I have to take my workspace apart to have a party."

"I love the designated space for my home office."

A client ran her very busy business from a table in an upstairs hallway alcove. She had to pack up every evening and store her files in a nearby guest room, which was beautifully decorated but rarely used. When I suggested that she set her office up permanently in the guest room and offer another room to her occasional guests, she was stunned: "I never thought of that." Like many people, she had put others first and "made do" for herself. We strategized how to set up her office in the guest room: the wrought iron four poster bed went to her thrilled daughter, her work table found a place by the window, and miscellaneous storage went into the closet. She now loves her designated home office space.

If this is your home office, this is the chapter for you. Looking beyond room labels opens up many options for home office space. A guest room, spare room, sunroom, dining room or even an unused living room can make a great home office when you are space-challenged. One client found moving his laptop from the coffee table to the dining table made a huge

A laptop on the coffee table is not a home office.

difference – no more creaking back pain after a day working on his computer.

When you create a designated space – even a simple but well thought-out space – for a task or activity, you have a greater chance of completing that task, doing that activity and meeting your goals.

Find a space that is large enough to meet your needs. Papers scattered in several different rooms is the number one reason for decreased efficiency in home offices. If your home office is too small you may find your work oozing into other rooms, like your dining room or bedroom.

Note: if you simply surf the web, answer personal emails and pay your bills online the need for a dedicated home office is not crucial.

A home office *ideally* has:
- at least 10x10 feet of floor space;
- a window;
- a door, if you need privacy;
- all necessary wiring and outlets;
- comfortable heating, cooling and ventilation;
- a private entrance if clients come to you, or if you have onsite staff;
- appropriate storage for your files and supplies.

You may be groaning or laughing at the above list because it does not represent your reality. If you have some or all of these features in your home office – fantastic. If you don't (and few of

> When you create a designated space for a task or activity, you have a greater chance of completing that task and meeting your goals.

Basements are dark and low energy - the worst place for you to work.

40

The desk and bookcase dominate this bedroom. It is not a restful retreat.

us do), this chapter will help you improvise and make the most of what you do have.

Home Office No-No's

I don't recommend an office in the basement. Basements can be dark, drab, damp places that will drag you down. If there is any other space in your home, put your office there.

Nor do I recommend home offices in your bedroom. Work papers or a computer sitting in the corner of your bedroom will beckon your subconscious to "do something!" when you are trying to sleep. This is a sadly effective way to undermine work/life boundaries.

Creative Use of Space

For many people a sofa bed or futon sofa allows an underused guest room to become a functional and pleasant home office. A Murphy Bed, which tips up and is stored in a tall cabinet or closet against the wall, can free up floor space. Modern inflatable beds now come with electric compressors. No more gasping for breath.

This Murphy Bed folds up into the wall cabinet.

Claiming un- or under-used spaces for your home office can be the solution to work space that is not meeting your needs or even hindering your work. Another client moved her office into her unused living room, as her family life and entertaining had moved into the new family room addition. She now enjoys lots of space and light, while she sees her children play in the back yard or they quietly

41

French doors create
semi-privacy.

A closet office gives you a
designated office in a small
space.

An office armoire is a
workspace incognito.

read on the sofa while she works. Meanwhile her children use her former tiny office near the kitchen as their computer and homework space.

If your lifestyle and entertaining are casual, you might convert an under-used dining room into your home office.

Some newer houses have a very small living room near the front door that is barely big enough for a love seat and two small chairs. It is isolated from the kitchen and family room and rarely used. That isolation from the active areas of the house makes it an excellent home office. Add a pair of doors for privacy, if needed. French doors allow light into your home office and the occasional glimpse out. You can add frosted glass windows or simple curtains to provide visual privacy. If you need sound-dampening from a noisy household then a solid-core or insulated door would be a better choice. Or you can use a white-noise machine, radio or fan to mask household or neighborhood noise.

When there is no spare or under-used room; then you need to be creative. Use the old fashioned pantry off your kitchen, remove the doors from a closet, or commandeer a space under the stairs. You can partition a corner with a folding screen, a bookcase perpendicular to the wall, or a row of tall potted plants. Or you can define your space with an area rug. By claiming and outlining your workspace with these objects, you will improve your focus. If you lack space and want to hide your workspace during personal time, an office armoire may be the best solution. Be sure it is tall enough so the top is above your head when you are sitting and the doors fold out of the way when it is open.

The Living Room Office

If your only option for workspace is your living room and you do not have room for an office armoire, then at least get your laptop off the coffee table. Use a small *adjustable* laptop table or snack table with "sled" feet that allow you to slide them under the sofa to bring the laptop closer to you. Or use a living room side table. For improved ergonomics, make sure your back is well supported – place a large pillow behind your back so you can sit up straight – and have a wrist rest cushion on the laptop table.

Highlights
- Look beyond room labels to reveal options for home office space.
- Home Office No-No's: Your home office in the basement or in your bedroom.
- Doors can be useful to establish boundaries and/or sound barriers.

Step #7
Storage Solutions:
Tips to Control the Paper Avalanche

"It doesn't file itself."

"There is not enough storage."

"Storage, storage, storage"

A client excitedly told me that after she organized her home office she felt more energized. "I was hoping to feel more efficient, but I did not expect to feel better in my office. If I had known this, I would have cleared out and set up my office sooner."

Clutter is Visual Noise

Many survey respondents wrote about their frustration with clutter and their need for an office organizing/paperwork system. Why is a minimally cluttered office so important? (Please note: I did not say "uncluttered.") If you have lots of stuff around, you keep thinking about what you need to do associated with that file, book or piece of mail. This leads to decreased focus, decreased productivity and decreased discretionary time. If you don't have to franticly search for a file or receipt, think of how much better your mood and your day will be: think of the time saved looking for something, or the money saved not replacing something mislaid.

Clutter is distracting.

Office Clutter comes in several forms:
- **Paper that comes into your home and never leaves** (junk mail, magazines, information pertinent to your business/field, announcements and ad infinitum).
- **Books that you have not looked at in years.**
- **Software and Data CDs** that are outdated.
- **Things you have "outgrown",** that belong to a previous job or former business goal.

Decluttering Creates New Energy

A cluttered office is a metaphor for no room in your life for new business and new opportunities. De-cluttering is like gardening: weeding out so there is room for things to grow and a future for you and your business. Even if you declutter a little at a time, file by file and drawer by drawer, you will feel a shift   in the energy in your space and that in turn will energize you.

> A cluttered office is a metaphor for no room in your life for new business and new opportunities.

Plan Your Decluttering with SPACE

Before you go out and get colorful little containers or spend thousands on a custom storage system do a few important steps first.

Julie Morgenstern, organization expert and author of the *Organizing from the Inside Out* series and other books, has developed an excellent approach to de-cluttering using **SPACE:** Sort, Purge, Assign, Containerize and Equalize.

S is for **Sort.** Start by sorting your stuff into five bins: keep, recycle, donate, repair, and trash. If you haven't used something within the last year, the chances of your using it in the next twelve months are slim to none.

P is for **Purge.** Let it go.

A is for **Assign a Home**. Place the things you use most often in the freed-up storage near your desk orin the now half-empty file drawer.

C is for **Containerize**. *Now* you can go shopping, because you know exactly what you need in files, shelves, bins and baskets.

E is for **Equalize.** The daily, weekly and monthly clear away and put away.

Organized people are not "better" people, just less stressed.

How long should you keep your financial records?

Julian Block, attorney and former IRS investigator, states that the IRS has three years to audit your return. Exceptions: If you did not file a return the IRS can come after you at any time. If you filed a return, but your real income was 25% greater than what you claimed, the Feds have six years to audit you. If you filed an accurate return, you can toss your receipts after 3 years. Julian Block suggests that you hold on to *all your tax return forms*, so you can prove to the IRS you *did* file.

Quick Starts to Organizing
Use the preschool model:
- Keep items near where they are used.
- Clean up and put away after you are done and before you move on to the next activity.
- Keep like items together: your printer paper and envelopes, all your software CDs.
- Store things so they are easy to see when you open a file drawer or cabinet.

The goal is ease and order, not perfection.

"Filing is for retrieval, not for storage."
- Karen McKenna-Veliotis, professional organizer

The Right File Cabinets and How to Make the Most of Them

You need file storage, even if you like to have most of your papers out and easy to see. The most efficient files have "full suspension" drawers. This means that the drawer can be pulled out completely and gives you easy access to items in the back of the drawer. Please don't be fooled like I was, "easy glide" drawers are not the same as "full suspension" file drawers. They do glide easily but they do not open all the way, so you have to grope for papers in the back third of the drawer. This kind of file is only two-thirds useful.

Full suspension file cabinets make filing and retrieving easier.

Be sure your file drawers have brackets for hanging folders or get suspension frames at an office supply store. This supports your files and makes them easy to see. Rather than having hanging folders overflowing, either divide the file into separate hanging folders and keep them together, or use a box bottom hanging file, with file folders inside to organize your papers.

Sort and declutter your file drawers. Have them no more than three-quarters full; this makes it easier to find your documents and put them back.

The Tickler File

Tickler files allow you to organize papers by due date. due.

A *tickler file* combines the functions of a file and a calendar. Set up a hanging folder for each month of the year and each day or week of the month. Place what you are currently working on in the file with the next day's date for easy retrieval tomorrow. Conference information can go in the designated month file. At the beginning of the month open the month file and place your notes, registration confirmations and tickets into the appropriate day's file. Then each morning you pull out the day file for the papers relating to what is on your calendar or to-do list. This can also be used to stash that perfect card until the birthday month arrives, or save travel information for an upcoming vacation.

Storage for Passwords and Usernames

Use a Rolodex™ to organize and store your internet passwords.

A well-respected author confessed his internet passwords are on slips of paper and sticky notes scattered around his desk. He knows that this isn't good but is stumped on how to keep and organize his password information. A rolodex-type file is perfect for this. When you sign up for a new website or forum, just pull out a card from the file and simply write the name of the group/web address and password and user name, and then pop the card into the right letter category. If office security is an issue, then use a horizontal rather than circular card file or a designated address book and keep it in a locked drawer.

The Proper Use of Bookcases

Bookcases are great for books, binders, magazines and other vertical items. But they are not all-purpose storage. They really don't work for all the miscellaneous "bits and bobs" of offices, like reams of paper, boxes of pencils, or floppy paper items like folders. Miscellaneous items do best in cabinets or the deeper shelves in a closet. Folders belong in file drawers or paper organizing bins. you need more bookcase storage but do not have the floor space, do what the Europeans do: "think tall." Rather than a three-shelf book case, use a six-shelf bookcase in the same space.

Think "tall" to store more in a small area. A six-shelf bookcase instead of a three-shelf bookcase.

Closets: The Hidden Star of Storage

If you are using a spare bedroom for your home office, the closet offers great opportunities for storage. Too often I see miscellaneous items crammed onto the single shelf above and a jumble of things on the floor below. To make the best use of this space install shelving for supplies such as boxes of pencils and envelopes, back-up CDs or reams of paper. A small file cabinet can be tucked in there, or store noisy and rarely used computer peripherals such as scanners or fax machines.

Shelves make closets more functional to store office supplies.

Visible Storage

Some of my clients don't feel comfortable with active files "hidden" in file cabinets; they want to have things out where they can see them. But you have only so much desktop space and don't want to start using the floor to stack papers. Visible filing may be the answer, but

Clear file bins for visible storage.

Wall mounted file holders for visual storage.

this needs some ingenuity. Mount shelves on a wall and line up *labeled* clear plastic boxes on the shelves. Lucite picture display boxes, placed face down on the shelf can be great for this. Or you can use the wall mounted file holders that you see in doctors' offices, either single file bins or the kind that come in a vertical row. Make sure these are labeled, kept up-to-date and not used as a dumping place for unresolved problems.

Idea Display for Visual Thinkers

Some people think visually to clarify issues and make decisions. A large wall calendar with enough white space for notes can be helpful in visualizing time when planning an event or working on deadline. A white board is perfect for mind-mapping, plotting business strategies or time-lining a project. Bulletin boards with pictures and charts can be another great use of wall space for inspiration and planning. Never use a bulletin board as a wall-mounted trash basket.

Labeling and bundling cords and cables makes for a safer and saner office..

Wire Management

I find it amazing that of all of the beautiful home offices shown in the media not a single one has wires or cables. These spaces are not designed for the real world. All your office electronics, even wireless gizmos, need to be charged or connected to your computer. This means wires and cables – not a pretty sight. Unfortunately most wire management options are not pretty either, but it is essential for safety and sanity.

51

- Label all cords and cables (near the plug) with plastic tags or "Post-It" flags re-enforced with clear adhesive tape.
- Coil cords together with velcro-type ties.
- Organize the tangle of recharging cords on your desktop for your laptop, PDA, cell phone or iPod with docking ports or cable clips.
- Bundle cords together into one compact "snake" in a corrugated plastic tube with a slit in the side.
- Attach cable trays or brackets below your desk to hold cables, power strips and modems off the floor.
- Mount cable raceways on the edge of your desktop (usually the side or back) or along your baseboard to hide connections to your phone, cable or electric outlet.

By corralling your cables and wires, your office will be neater, safer and there will be room to put your feet under your desk (good ergonomics). LifeHacker.com ("hacker" as in solving a problem in a clever way, not as in internet criminal) has some great wire management ideas under "DYI".

Attractive Camouflage for Wires

If you have positioned your desk perpendicular to a wall, you will probably have a cascade of wires going down the back or side or your desk. The above wire management gadgets can help bundle these cords together, but you may be left with that unsightly cable bundle. Consider placing a re-purposed fireplace

A re-purposed fireplace screen camouflages unsightly wires.

screen, short folding screen or potted floor plant at the back of your desk to offer attractive camouflage.

Plan a Smooth Exit

Create a landing zone/launch pad in your home office. A designated space for your briefcase, purse or laptop bag and any papers, books or other things you bring home with you or need ready to grab-and-go. This can be a basket, a shelf, a coat hook or drawer near the door.

Take five minutes to clear off your desk and straighten up your office at the end of the day, every work day. Put your current project in the appropriate folder or tickler file. Think of how you want to enter your office tomorrow with a sense of order and positive anticipation of the day ahead, not as if you are entering a chaotic "black hole." Schedule a weekly 15-minute session to dust, vacuum and wipe down your office. These short bursts of clearing and cleaning help to prevent "The Big De-clutter." Having a messy, disorganized office saps your energy and makes you dread working in your home office.

An organized home office, where space is cleared and similar things are grouped together, not only feels calmer but looks more spacious.

Highlights
- Clutter is visual noise, a source of distractions and confusion.
- Plan your de-cluttering with "SPACE".
- Use "full-suspension" file cabinets.
- Consider using a "tickler file" to organize papers by due dates.
- Think tall.
- Use visual storage wisely.
- Coil, bundle and camouflage your wires.
- Take five minutes at the end of your work day to clear your desk and prepare for tomorrow.
- The goal is ease and order, not perfection.

Step # 8
The Fun Part:
Add Inspiration with Beauty and
Personal Mementos to Increase Productivity

**A Boring Office Is Just As
Counter-Productive As A Messy Office.**

"It's not inviting."

"I need a place to put personal things."

"It's utilitarian. It's not set up right. I don't know how."

After seven chapters on how to create a functional and comfortable office, we come to the fun part: personalizing and adding beauty to your workspace. This is not some exercise in frippery, but the important final step of fine-tuning your workspace and enhancing productivity through personal inspiration.

How Environmental Stimulation Impacts Personal Productivity

Noisy co-workers and machines, boring beige cubicles, blasts of frigid air or stifling heat, and people moving past your desk – these are some of the forms of environmental stimuli you encounter in the business world. In a corporate office you have little or no control over the amount of stimulation you experience, which in itself is a source of stress. In your home office you have more influence over the amount and kind of stimulation around you.

A boring office is just as counter-productive as a cluttered office.

Studies show that environmental stimulation directly impacts your concentration and productivity. *Environmental stimulation* is science speak for light, color, textures, sounds, movement and decoration. At the peak of the bell curve is the "comfort zone" or "sweet spot" of maximum productivity. Too little stimulation and people worked slower. Too much stimulation and test subjects were distracted and their output dropped off.

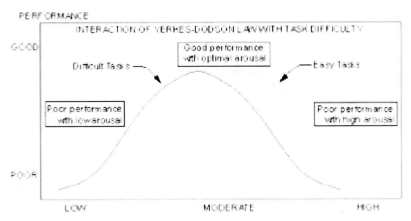

Peak performance occurs at the personal midpoint between too little (boring) and too much (overwhelming) environmental stimulation.
- Yerkes and Dodson

Use this information to fine-tune your office for the best level of stimulation to improve your focus and efficiency. Decorating an office is not a one-size-fits-all affair. The ideal level of stimulation varies from person to person, even from task to task. What makes an office "exciting" for one person may be experienced by another as "tense"; what is "serene" for one can be perceived by another as "boring."

The second bell curve on the right demonstrates that people who did rote tasks, or activities with a lot of repetition, needed *more* environmental stimulation. This means that when you are stuffing envelopes or similar tasks that do not require mental focus, you will do better if there is more stimulation in your environment, such as up-beat music. When stimulation/decoration support you and your work, it becomes a very personal form of beauty.

56

Sources of Stimulation and Beauty for the Workspace

It is important to find the level of stimulation that creates your comfort zone – what is neither too overwhelming nor too boring. Do you function best with a lot or a little visual stimulation? Do you feel most focused in a space with little or no decoration, something very spare? Or do you feel most comfortable with reminders of your life around you, such as photos of friends and family or a collection of memorabilia? Some people need absolute silence when they work, while others need the sounds of life around them. This changes from task to task: Writing or focused analysis needs one level of stimulation, while stuffing envelopes or artisan work will need more stimulation (no matter what your baseline is). There is no *one* right way; the best way is what is right for *you*.

There are several categories of stimulation that you can use to fine-tune your workspace to create your own "comfort zone" of environmental input. They are: visual, auditory, tactile, kinetic and temperature.

Music, color, and texture are some of the forms of environmental stimulation you can use in your home office.

Visual includes colors for walls, floors and furniture, as well as artwork, photos and mementos. Step back and look at your office as a whole and determine what takes up most of your visual field. Use wall colors as background for your decor.

Auditory: Music is an overlooked source of beauty in our lives. A radio, a CD or MP3 player, or streaming audio from your computer is a great way to bring this into your work space. If you share a workspace, then headphones or ear buds are the answers. But be aware of distracting sound "overflow" if you pump up the volume.

Use decorative elements or accessories made of natural materials.

Tactile: If your office furniture is made of laminates, metal and synthetic fabrics, use decorative elements or accessories made of natural materials to offset the coldness of artificial materials. Instead of an ordinary coffee mug as your pencil holder, use a beautifully crafted wood or handmade pottery container. Your local art fair or open studio event will have wonderful things to choose from. Add a rug for color, texture and pattern. (If the rug goes under your desk chair get a chair mat.)

Kinetic: Movement in your space such as mobiles, a curtain rippling in a breeze, fish swimming in an aquarium, or the glimpse of a flag or flowers fluttering in the wind are all forms of kinetic energy. Movement is also space to walk around in while you think or talk on the phone.

Temperature: Being too hot or cold is distracting. I have seen both personal fans and fingerless gloves used in the same corporate office. In your home office you can adjust the thermostat, air conditioner, or space heater for your comfort and maximum alertness. Even better – you can open a window.

We will discuss the many ways you can use decoration and personalization in your home office to create the "sweet spot" of stimulation for your work needs.

Personalize Your Office for Focused Mental Work with Little Physical Activity

To create an office that supports focused mental work, you want to avoid both over-stimulation that leads to distraction as well as minimalist boredom that leads to restlessness or drowsiness.

Colors: Neutrals or blues and greens in a mid-range to dark tone support mental focus. Avoid spaces with dramatic contrasts in color. An all-white or all-beige room will bore you to distraction and lead to daydreaming. Red (except for a few well-chosen accents) will stimulate physical action rather than mental focus.

Tactile: Subtle textures and harmonious and symmetric patterns will not distract you.

Lighting: Medium level lighting with dimmer light around the edges of the room. "Warm White" lighting is especially important to support memory and problem-solving tasks.

> In decoration, over-stimulation can lead to distraction, while extreme minimalism can cause boredom.

Sound: Listen to nature sounds or music that is slower, harmonious and consistent in tempo and volume. Choose harmonious music such as soft jazz, Baroque, Bach and Mozart, all at quiet volume. Very few people require total silence to do analytical work.

Decoration: You can choose a simple decor or arrange decorative elements with generous empty wall space in between to rest your eyes and your mind.

For Active Work that Requires Less Mental Focus and More Physical Activity: For repetitive work or artisan work, a workspace with more stimulation gets you energized to do physically focused work, draw yourself out of your thoughts and avoid boredom.

Colors: Try moderately bright colors, especially warm colors like yellow, orange and red.

Tactile: Use varied textures in more complex, asymmetric and geometric patterns.

Lighting: Bright levels of light help to energize a space and make detailed handwork easier to see and do.

Sounds: Listen to up-beat music with variations in tempo such as Beethoven, rock, reggae, disco and opera, all at a moderately loud volume.

Minimal decoration is the comfort zone for some people who do focused mental work.	An abundance of personalization with organization provides the stimulation needed by other people.

Place your inspirations nearby.

Decoration: Your walls and shelves can be filled with pictures and memorabilia.

If cold calls or telephone outreach are part of your work life, set up your office for the quieter environment of mental-focus and then play rockin' music to pump yourself up before you call. Place something stimulating, like a red file folder, on your desk while you are on the phone. When you are finished with your cold calls, put the red folder away, turn on your quieter music to unwind and prepare for your paperwork.

Beauty and Fun in Your Home Office

"Books and art make the most personal statement."
– Rose Tarlow, decorator and entrepreneur.

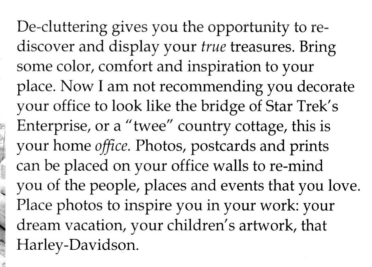

De-cluttering gives you the opportunity to re-discover and display your *true* treasures. Bring some color, comfort and inspiration to your place. Now I am not recommending you decorate your office to look like the bridge of Star Trek's Enterprise, or a "twee" country cottage, this is your home *office.* Photos, postcards and prints can be placed on your office walls to re-mind you of the people, places and events that you love. Place photos to inspire you in your work: your dream vacation, your children's artwork, that Harley-Davidson.

Add something for the sheer beauty of it. Hang a relaxing picture on the wall beyond your computer screen, this way you can look up and take a mini-mental break. Ideally it should be a picture with depth or perspective so you look

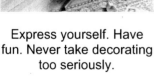

Express yourself. Have fun. Never take decorating too seriously.

into the picture, thereby changing the focus of your eyes for a minute and decreasing eye fatigue.

Please do not shop for artwork at box stores. It may be convenient, but the art there is bland and generic. Check out online sites for more inspiring art and photographs. Your local newspaper may have photos of your town or local sports teams for sale. Check your favorite museum or alumni association. Enlarge and frame a favorite snapshot.

If something no longer lifts your spirits, it is OK to let it go. We are all growing and changing. Make room for new inspirations.

It is not necessary to cover your walls with art and photos like wallpaper. Allow for some blank spaces on your walls and horizontal surfaces. Just as a sip of water is a palate cleanser during a rich meal; a bit of empty wall space is a visual palate cleanser to help you focus and think.

"Don't crowd your home right away.
leave space for the journey that you're going to take."
- Marcus Samuelsson, chef, restauranteur and collector.

Decorate and personalize your
home office with photos of
your dream vacation, your dream home
or your children's artwork.

Highlights

- A boring office is just as counter-productive as a messy office.

- Environmental stimulation impacts personal productivity.

- Decorating an office is not a one-size-fits-all affair.

- Fine-tuning your office for the best level of stimulation will improve your focus and efficiency.

- Use a variety of sources of stimulation and beauty in your workspace.

- Decorate your office to support focused mental work, telephone sales work, or active physical work with different colors, textures and sounds.

- Personalize your home office for beauty, fun and inspiration.

Postscript
The Dilemma of the Home Office: Distractions and Isolation

The Home Office Vending Machine

"I need better work/life boundaries."

"It is too easy to get pulled into stuff around the house."

"My office is at the other end of the house. It is lonely there."

A unique response to the survey had me laughing out loud: "My home office needs a vending machine." But the more I thought about it, the more I realized the wished-for vending machine can be more than a dispenser of food. It represents the need for a break from monotony and a chance to connect, even briefly, with others.

Among the candid responses to my survey, I was surprised by the number of comments about too many distractions when working at home or how working at home is isolating. On reflection, it became clear that **the common solution for both distractions and isolation is the need for strong yet permeable work-life boundaries.** Coping with too many distractions means reinforcing your defined workspace and work hours, while scheduling breaks to cope with life. Coping with isolation means cutting holes in your enforced isolation with breaks to get out of your office and see a bit of world (or at least your neighborhood.)

Distractions come in many forms.

There are limits to multi-tasking.

Distractions

For most people too many distractions come from family and family commitments. Explain to your family that when you are in your office or at your desk, you are working and should not be disturbed. Be consistent with this. If you were working in an office away from home they would not be able to ask for your attention every other minute.

But you don't need a family to be distracted by the telephone (screen your calls for urgency), email (turn off your email alarm and check your email at predetermined times, such as mid-morning, noon and late afternoon. If it is a real emergency they will call you.), or the siren call of the refrigerator (stash healthy snacks in your office or in a designated space in your refrigerator to prevent grazing.)

Set up physical boundaries with a closed door or a "Do Not Disturb, Mom at Work" sign. Background music or a white noise machine can help mask household noise. Have your own computer, rather than try to claim time on a "family" computer. Have a dedicated phone number for your business. Don't answer the house phone line – you would not hear it if you worked in a conventional office. Give your child's school your office and cell phone number for emergencies, just like any working parent. Ask family and friends to call you on your cell only if it is urgent; otherwise they should call the house number and you will get back to them later.

Plan for breaks from work to spend time with your children, such as snack time, and check-in with your kids when they get home from school. Then set them up with things they can do to entertain themselves, with the reassurance you will be with them again when you are preparing dinner. If your children are too young to be on their own then plan for child care in the form of a baby sitter, after-school program, extended pre-school, or trade child care time with a neighbor. Praise your children and spouse generously when they respect your work boundaries. Then make a point of taking the time to cheer on their jump shots, artwork or accomplishments.

If your children want to be near you while you work and can play or read quietly, set up a play area or a sofa/love seat in your office for them.

Take breaks and connect with others.

Sometimes even a closed door will not stop a determined child or oblivious partner from interrupting you. A friend with three young sons, who needed focused time alone on a regular basis, taught them, "Don't disturb Mommy unless the house is on fire or one of you is bleeding." And it worked! *Most* of the time.

Isolation

Working at home can be lonely, after the thrill of working in your pajamas and slippers wanes. As a human being you are a social creature and need *connection*, not mere contact, with others. Build breaks into your day. These will need to be more consciously planned than a walk to the vending machine, but they are just as important.

Take breaks to replenish your tired brain. Go for a walk or to the gym; you will return to work refreshed and ready to focus again. Go to a coffee shop and reward yourself with your favorite latté.

Take a break from working at home and bring your laptop or papers with you and savor your coffee while working with other people around you. You can work at your local library as many now have wireless internet access.

Take a people break. Walk with an exercise partner, daily. Meet with colleagues for lunch or tea on a weekly basis. Join a professional organization or two to get out, socialize and learn more about your field. Breaking out of the isolation of working at home takes a more conscious effort, but the rewards are connection when you want, with the people you like. Plan on having a voice-to-voice or face-to-face interaction with at least one adult today – email just does not cut it for real human connection.

Don't get trapped by your work life.

The issue of distractions and isolation is complex. It involves reinforcing physical and time boundaries or breaking through them. Just as setting-up a home office is not a one-size-fits-all proposition, there is no one solution for everyone. Try different ideas and see which one works best for you.

Work/life Boundaries are Essential for Your Sanity and Efficiency

If you work at home, it is especially important that you create mental and physical boundaries between your work life and your personal life. It is too easy to have work overtake your entire existence. To support your mental boundaries and signal the end of your work day, leave your office picked up and close the door. One client developed a little ritual of mindfully closing the appointment book on her desk. Another client found an antique open/closed sign and consciously turned it to "closed" when he stopped work for the day.

Action Plan:
How to Create the Best Home Office
For Your Work Style, Step-by-Step

If several ideas in the previous chapters have inspired you to make improvements in your office, here is a brief listing (in chronological order) of the key concepts in *The Smarter Home Office*.

- Dinosaur Space: Look around to see if there is underused or overlooked space you can use to support your work life. (If you have a designated office, skip this step.)

- De-clutter, organize and set up storage.

- Color: Consider painting your office for improved focus or stimulation, or to simply refresh your space.

- Position your desk, bookcases, files and reading chair to enhance work flow.

- Adjust your computer monitor or laptop, keyboard and chair for optimal ergonomics.

- Set up lighting for your desk, your reading chair and to provide a second source of light in your space.

- Nature: Maximize your views and bring natural elements into your office.

- Personalize your office with photos, mementos and music. Select them to support the level of environmental stimulation you need for your work style.

You enter your revitalized office and see sunlight illuminating your desk. You sit down and relax knowing your chair, monitor and keyboard are adjusted for sustained support and comfort. You turn on music and reach into a nearby file for today's paperwork. Glancing out the window you see the sky and a thriving potted plant brings nature closer to you. On the wall are pictures that remind you of who and what you love most. A comfortable chair awaits you when you need a break from your desk. Your office supports you and your work style for increased income, inspiration and comfort.

Photo credits

Cover Photo: © istockphoto/flashon
Page 1: cc Jeremy Levine Design
Page 2: cc___, cc Fabio Bruna
Page 7: © istockphoto/e-rasmus
Page 8: ___ , cc crschmidt, © Crate & Barrel
Page 9: © Crate & Barrel, © istockphoto/laughingmango, © istockphoto/Ron Bailey
Page 10: ___ , © CoolestGadgets.ca
Page 13: ___ , ____, © Ali Edward
Page 15: © istockphoto/motoed
Page 16: cc Hanford.gov
Page 17: ___, © istockphoto/, © IKEA
Page 18: © istockphoto/
Page 19: © Standupdesks.com
Page 20: cc Hanford.gov, © istockphoto/futek
Page 21: cc Bolshakov
Page 24: © istockphoto/blackred
Page 25: cc aldenchadwick
Page 26: cc WikiMedia
Page 29: cc foxspain
Page 30: cc KayCey97007, © BudgetBlindsmfgltd.com
Page 31: cc kretyan, cc Claudio Matsuoka, cc chrismichaels
Page 41: cc Jeremy Levine Design, © Murphy Bed Sales
Page 42: cc ckelly, cc_____, © Highgate Furniture, UK
Page 45: cc Kai Hendry
Page 48: © __ , photo by author
Page 49: © rolodex
Page 50: © furniture123.co.uk, ____ , © stampinpretty
Page 51: © kitchen-plus.com,
Page 55: cc Malcolm Tredinnick
Page 56: © Abel Cheng
Page 57: cc Fabio Bruna, cc maticulous
Page 60: cc Jeremy Levine Design, cc moriza
Page 61: cc milesgehm, cc back garage
Page 62: cc tristrambrelstaff
Page 65: cc Official PSDS.com
Page 66: © istockphoto/killerb10
Page 67: cc roland
Page 68: © istockphoto/joshblake
Author photo: © Lynn McCann

(cc) "cc" means "creative commons":copyright-free creative works than can be reproduced with attribution.

About the Author

Linda Varone, MA is an award-winning home and office design consultant, named Best of Boston® by Boston magazine. She has been helping people add warmth, energy and comfort to their spaces since 1991, using a unique blend of interior design and architectural psychology: the subtle yet powerful impact the structure and design of a space has on people's comfort level. Linda uses her expertise to help clients create offices that support focus, productivity and personal inspiration.

As a professional speaker, Linda has shared her practical, content-rich approach to design with enthusiastic audiences nationwide, including: Fortune 500 Forum, Harvard University, IKEA, Institute for Healthcare Improvement, BuildBoston and Yankee Dental Conference.

Linda has had articles published on Entrepreneur.com and has been frequently quoted in the Boston Globe and Boston magazine.

Contact Linda
- To order books,
- Book a personal consultation or,
- To arrange a presentation for your company or organization.

Linda@TheSmarterHomeOffice.com
Or www.TheSmarterHomeOffice.com

9 780984 404506